Sand Creek Massacre National Historic Site
Final Acoustical Monitoring Report

Natural Resource Technical Report NPS/NRSS/NRTR—2011/475

Emma Lynch
Natural Sounds and Night Skies Division
National Park Service
1201 Oakridge Drive, Suite 100
Fort Collins, CO 80525

August 2011

U.S. Department of the Interior
National Park Service
Natural Resource Stewardship and Science
Fort Collins, Colorado

The National Park Service, Natural Resource Stewardship and Science office in Fort Collins, Colorado publishes a range of reports that address natural resource topics of interest and applicability to a broad audience in the National Park Service and others in natural resource management, including scientists, conservation and environmental constituencies, and the public.

The Natural Resource Technical Report Series is used to disseminate results of scientific studies in the physical, biological, and social sciences for both the advancement of science and the achievement of the National Park Service mission. The series provides contributors with a forum for displaying comprehensive data that are often deleted from journals because of page limitations.

All manuscripts in the series receive the appropriate level of peer review to ensure that the information is scientifically credible, technically accurate, appropriately written for the intended audience, and designed and published in a professional manner.

Data in this report were collected and analyzed using methods based on established, peer-reviewed protocols and were analyzed and interpreted within the guidelines of the protocols.

Views, statements, findings, conclusions, recommendations, and data in this report do not necessarily reflect views and policies of the National Park Service, U.S. Department of the Interior. Mention of trade names or commercial products does not constitute endorsement or recommendation for use by the U.S. Government.

This report is available from [Natural Sounds and Night Skies Division, http://www.nature.nps.gov/naturalsounds/] and the Natural Resource Publications Management website (http://www.nature.nps.gov/publications/nrpm/).

Please cite this publication as:

Lynch, E., 2011. Sand Creek Massacre National Historic Site: Final acoustical monitoring report. Natural Resource Technical Report NPS/NRSS/NRTR—2011//475. National Park Service, Fort Collins, Colorado.

NPS 042/109120, August 2011

Contents

	Page
Figures	v
Tables	vi
Executive Summary	vii
List of Terms	ix
Introduction	1
National Park Service Natural Sounds Program	1
Soundscape Monitoring and Planning Authorities	1
Study Area	5
Methods	7
Equipment	7
Monitoring period	7
Calculation of Metrics	7
Calculation of diel L_x values	8
Off-Site Sound Source Analysis	8
On-Site Listening	9
Results	11
On-site listening	11
Off site analysis	13
Metrics	15
Conclusion	19
Literature Cited	21
Appendix A: Visual analysis	23
Appendix B: Glossary of Acoustical Terms	25

Figures

Page

Figure 1. SAND001 acoustical monitoring site during winter monitoring. Looking westward. 5

Figure 2. Location of SAND001 6

Figure 3. An acoustical technician uses software to visually analyze type and duration of sound sources. 9

Figure 4. An acoustical technician tracks audible sound sources on a PDA during an on-site listening session. 10

Figure 5. Median hourly exceedence metrics in dBA at SAND001 summer. 16

Figure 6. Median hourly exceedence metrics in dBA at SAND001 winter 16

Figure 7. Day and night dB levels for 33 one-third octave bands at SAND001 summer 17

Figure 8. Day and night dB levels for 33 one-third octave bands at SAND001 winter 18

Figure 9. A demonstration of visual noise source analysis, using SPL annotation tool (SPLAT). 23

Tables

Page

Table 1. Explanation of sound level values vii

Table 2. Percent time above metrics for summer and winter. viii

Table 3. Metadata for each season of acoustical monitoring. 5

Table 4. Summary of data collected at SAND from 2009-2011 11

Table 5. Summary of on-site audible sources for one hour at SAND001 summer. n=1. 12

Table 6. Summary of on-site audible sources for one hour at SAND001 winter. n=4. 12

Table 7. Summary of off-site analysis for audible sound sources, SAND001 summer. n=8. 14

Table 8. Summary of off-site analysis for audible sound sources, SAND001 winter. n=8. 14

Executive Summary

This report presents acoustical data that were collected by the National Park Service Natural Sounds Program at Sand Creek Massacre National Historic Site between 2009 and 2011. Data were collected to provide park managers with information about the acoustical environment, noise sources, and to provide an estimate of natural ambient sound levels throughout the park. This information will in turn be used to help park managers, planners, and tribal representatives develop desired conditions for soundscapes in the park's first general management plan (GMP). Data will also inform decision makers about the potential impacts of noise from military jets during the Colorado Air National Guard's (COANG) National Environmental Policy Act (NEPA) process for the proposed expansion of the Cheyenne Military Operations Area.

Long-term acoustical monitoring was performed in two halves (summer and winter) in order to document seasonal variation. Each time, the Natural Sounds Program (NSP) deployed a sound level meter which collected 1 second L_{eq} data for thirty-three 1/3-octave bands. Each system contained meteorological sensors which collected temperature, relative humidity, wind speed, and wind direction. A continuous recorder was also simultaneously deployed to document sound sources. Overall, existing ambient sound levels ranged from about 15.4 dBA to 30.2 dBA in the winter and 29.6 dBA to 37.6 dBA in the summer. The difference in sound levels between winter and summer were anticipated, as biologic activity is generally reduced in the winter. Sound source analysis of these two datasets reveals that noise is audible in the National Historic Site between 33 and 36 percent of the time in both winter and summer. The most common source of noise during both seasons was commercial jet overflights. Natural sources such as wind in vegetation, birds, and insects were also commonly audible.

When determining the current conditions of an acoustical environment, it is important to be familiar with the acoustical terms used in this report, and to examine how often sound levels exceed certain values. Table 1 summarizes sound level values that relate to human health and speech, as documented in the scientific literature. These values are relevant to various aspects of the park experience including: camping in front-country and back-country sites, communication between park staff and visitors, and informal communication. Human responses can serve as a proxy for potential impacts to other vertebrates because humans have more sensitive hearing at low frequencies than most species (Dooling and Popper, 2007). Table 2 lists results for these four relevant values. Results indicate that existing ambient sound levels rarely exceeded 45 dBA in the summer, and 35 dBA in the winter.

Table 1. Explanation of sound level values

Sound Levels (dBA)	Relevance
35	Blood pressure and heart rate increase in sleeping humans (Haralabidis et al., 2008)
45	World Health Organization's recommendation for maximum noise levels inside bedrooms (Berglund, Lindvall, and Schwela, 1999)
52	Speech interference for interpretive programs (U.S. Environmental Protection Agency, 1974)
60	Speech interruption for normal conversation (U.S. Environmental Protection Agency, 1974)

Table 2. Percent time above metrics for summer and winter.

Site	Frequency Range (Hz)	% Time above sound level: 0700 to 1900				% Time above sound level: 1900 to 0700			
		35dBA	45dBA	52dBA	60dBA	35 dBA	45dBA	52 dBA	60 dBA
SAND001 Summer	12.5-20,000	74.1	21.1	6.3	0.9	42.2	6.8	1.7	0.1
SAND001 Winter	12.5-20,000	9.8	0.5	0.1	0.0	1.6	0.1	0.0	0.0

For reference, a list of commonly used acoustical terms is provided below. A more complete glossary can be found in Appendix B.

List of Terms

The table below lists a number of terms that may be used in this report.

Term	Definition
Acoustical Environment	The actual physical sound resources, regardless of audibility, at a particular location.
A-weighted sound pressure level in decibels (dB(A) or dBA)	A frequency-based methodology used to account for changes in human hearing sensitivity as a function of frequency. The A-weighting network de-emphasizes the high (6.3 kHz and above) and low (below 1 kHz) frequencies, and emphasizes the frequencies between 1 and 6.3 kHz, in an effort to simulate the relative response of the human ear. A-weighted decibels are defined as ten times the logarithm to the base ten of the ratio of A-weighted squared sound pressure to the squared reference sound pressure of 20 µPa, the squared sound pressure being obtained with fast (F) (125-ms) exponentially weighted time averaging. Alternatively, slow (S) (1000-ms) exponentially weighted time averaging may be specified.
Decibel	Decibel is abbreviated dB, and is a logarithmic unit of sound-pressure-squared level; it is common practice, however, to shorten this to sound pressure level, when no ambiguity results from so doing. 0 dB represents the lowest sound level that can be perceived by a human with healthy hearing. The formula for computing decibels is: $L_{db} = 10\log_{10}(P_1/P_0)$
Existing ambient	The composite, all-inclusive sound associated with a given environment, excluding only the analysis system's electrical noise (i.e., both extrinsic and intrinsic sounds are included).
Extrinsic Sound	Any sound not forming an essential part of the park unit, or a sound originating from outside the park boundary (also see Intrinsic Sound).
Frequency	Frequency equals the speed of sound divided by wavelength, and can be expressed in cycles per second, or Hertz (Hz). For a function periodic in time, the frequency is the reciprocal of the period, where the period is the smallest increment of an independent variable for which a function repeats itself (also see Hertz).
Hertz (Hz)	A measure of frequency, or the number of pressure variations per second. A person with normal hearing can hear between 20 Hz and 20,000 Hz. Kilohertz (kHz) equals 1000 Hz.
Intrinsic sound	A sound which belongs to a park by its very nature, based on the park unit purposes, values, and establishing legislation. The term "intrinsic sounds" has replaced "natural sounds" in order to incorporate both cultural and historic sounds as part of the acoustic environment of a park (also see Extrinsic Sound).
L_{eq}	Energy Equivalent Sound Level. The level of a constant sound over a specific time period that has the same sound energy as the actual (unsteady) sound over the same period.
L_x (exceedence level)	The A-weighted sound level equal to or exceeded by a fluctuating sound level x percent of a stated time period. For example, the symbol L10 represents that sound level which is exceeded 10 percent of the stated time period.
Natural ambient	The natural sound conditions found in a study area, including all sounds of nature (i.e., wind, streams, wildlife, etc.), and excluding all human and mechanical sounds.
Noise	Sound which is unwanted, either because of its effects on humans, its effect on fatigue or malfunction of physical equipment, or its interference with the perception or detection of other

	sounds.[1]
Percent Time Audible (PA)	The percent of time that a time-varying sound level may be detected in the presence of ambient sound as audible by the human ear.
Spectrum -- 1/3 octave	Acoustic intensity measurements in a sequence of spectral bands that span 1/3 octave. The International Standards Organization defines 1/3rd octave bands used by most sound level meters (ISO 266, 1975). 1/3rd octave frequency bands approximate the auditory filter widths of the human peripheral auditory system.
Sound pressure level	Ten times the logarithm to the base ten of the ratio of the time-mean-square pressure of a sound, in a stated frequency band, to the square of the reference sound pressure in gases of 20 μPa, the threshold of human hearing. SPL = $10\text{Log}_{10}(p^2/p_{ref}^2)$, where p^2 = time-mean-square sound pressure and p_{ref}^2 = squared reference sound pressure of 20 μPa.

[1] McGraw Hill Dictionary of Scientific and Technical Terms, online
http://www.accessscience.com/index.aspx

Introduction

The purpose of this report is to present acoustical data that were collected at Sand Creek Massacre National Historic Site in the winter of 2011. These data were collected to quantify various aspects of the acoustical environment thereby providing information that can be applied to park management decisions and planning efforts. This report synthesizes the results from two data collection efforts by presenting figures, tables, and descriptions of the data; it does not attempt to make recommendations or draw management conclusions.

A 1998 survey of the American public revealed that 72 percent of respondents thought that providing opportunities to experience natural quiet and the sounds of nature was a very important reason for having national parks, while another 23 percent thought that it was somewhat important (Haas & Wakefield 1998). In another survey specific to park visitors, 91 percent of respondents considered enjoyment of natural quiet and the sounds of nature as compelling reasons for visiting national parks (McDonald et al. 1995). In response to the value placed on experiencing the sounds of nature by visitors and the importance of the acoustic environment in park ecosystems, NPS policy states that park managers will protect, preserve, and restore park soundscapes in a manner that will leave them unimpaired for future generations. Acoustical monitoring provides a scientific basis for assessing the current status of acoustic resources, identifying trends in resource conditions, quantifying impacts from other actions, assessing consistency with park management objectives and standards, and informing management decisions regarding desired future conditions.

National Park Service Natural Sounds Program

The NPS Natural Sounds Program (NSP) was established in 2000 to help parks manage sounds in a way that protects park resources and is consistent with the expectations of park visitors. In 2010, the NSP became part of the new Natural Sounds and Night Skies Division of the National Park Service.

The NSP works to protect, maintain, or restore acoustical environments throughout the National Park System. Program staff work in partnership with parks and others to increase scientific understanding and inspire public appreciation of the value and character of soundscapes. NSP measures the acoustic environment in parks by conducting acoustic monitoring, data collection in parks; analyses acoustic data to characterize and describe acoustic conditions; assists parks in identifying, assessing, and addressing noise intrusions; and provides technical, planning, and policy guidance to ensure that the acoustic environment is protected for future generations.

Soundscape Monitoring and Planning Authorities

The National Park Service Organic Act of 1916 states that the purpose of national parks is "… to conserve the scenery and the natural and historic objects and the wild life therein and to provide for the enjoyment of the same in such manner and by such means as will leave them unimpaired for the enjoyment of future generations." In addition to the NPS Organic Act, the Redwoods Act of 1978 affirmed that, "the protection, management, and administration of these areas shall be conducted in light of the high value and integrity of the National Park System and shall not be exercised in derogation of the values and purposes for which these various areas have been established, except as may have been or shall be directly and specifically provided by Congress."

Direction for management of natural soundscapes[2] is represented in 2006 Management Policy 4.9:

> The Service will restore to the natural condition wherever possible those park soundscapes that have become degraded by unnatural sounds (noise), and will protect natural soundscapes from unacceptable impacts. Using appropriate management planning, superintendents will identify what levels and types of unnatural sound constitute acceptable impacts on park natural soundscapes. The frequencies, magnitudes, and durations of acceptable levels of unnatural sound will vary throughout a park, being generally greater in developed areas. In and adjacent to parks, the Service will monitor human activities that generate noise that adversely affects park soundscapes [acoustic resources], including noise caused by mechanical or electronic devices. The Service will take action to prevent or minimize all noise that through frequency, magnitude, or duration adversely affects the natural soundscape [acoustic resource] or other park resources or values, or that exceeds levels that have been identified through monitoring as being acceptable to or appropriate for visitor uses at the sites being monitored (NPS 2006a).

It should be noted that NPS Management Policies state "the natural ambient sound level—that is, the environment of sound that exists in the absence of human-caused noise—is the baseline condition, and the standard against which current conditions in a soundscape [acoustic resource] will be measured and evaluated" (NPS 2006b). However, the appropriate acoustic baseline and acceptable impacts may also depend upon the resources and the values of the park. For instance, "culturally appropriate sounds are important elements of the national park experience in many parks" (NPS 2006b). In this case, "the Service will preserve soundscape resources and values of the parks to the greatest extent possible to protect opportunities for appropriate transmission of cultural and historic sounds that are fundamental components of the purposes and values for which the parks were established" (NPS 2006b). A glossary of acoustical terms can be found in Appendix B.

According to NPS policy, best available scientific data must serve as the foundation of park management, decision making, and planning. NPS Management Policies states "Decision-makers and planners will use the best available scientific and technical information and scholarly analysis to identify appropriate management actions for protection and use of park resources…Decisions about the extent and degree of management actions taken to protect or restore park ecosystems or their components will be based on clearly articulated, well-supported

---

[2] The 2006 Management Policy 4.9 and related documents refer to "soundscapes" instead of "acoustic resources." When quoting from this authority, it is advisable to note that the term often refers to resources rather than visitor perceptions.

management objectives and the best scientific information available." The Management Policies further state that collection of relevant data is necessary for science-based decision making: "The collection and analysis of information about park resources will be a continuous process that will help ensure that decisions are consistent with park purposes." This report summarizes acoustic data collected in SAND in order to inform park decision making, management and planning.

Study Area

One acoustical monitoring system was deployed during the summer of 2009 for 45 days and the winter of 2011 for 32 days. This site was selected to serve as the monitoring location for both seasons because it was representative of the dominant vegetation, and therefore, the acoustical environment within the park.

Table 3. Metadata for each season of acoustical monitoring.

Site	Site Name	Dates Deployed	Vegetation	Elevation	Latitude	Longitude
SAND001	Massacre Site	7/13/09 - 8/26/09	Blue grama w/ sage. Near riparian area.	1208m	38.55259	102.50508
SAND001	Massacre Site	1/13/11 - 2/14/11	Blue grama w/ sage. Near riparian area.	1208m	38.55259	102.50508

Figure 1. SAND001 acoustical monitoring site during winter monitoring. Looking westward.

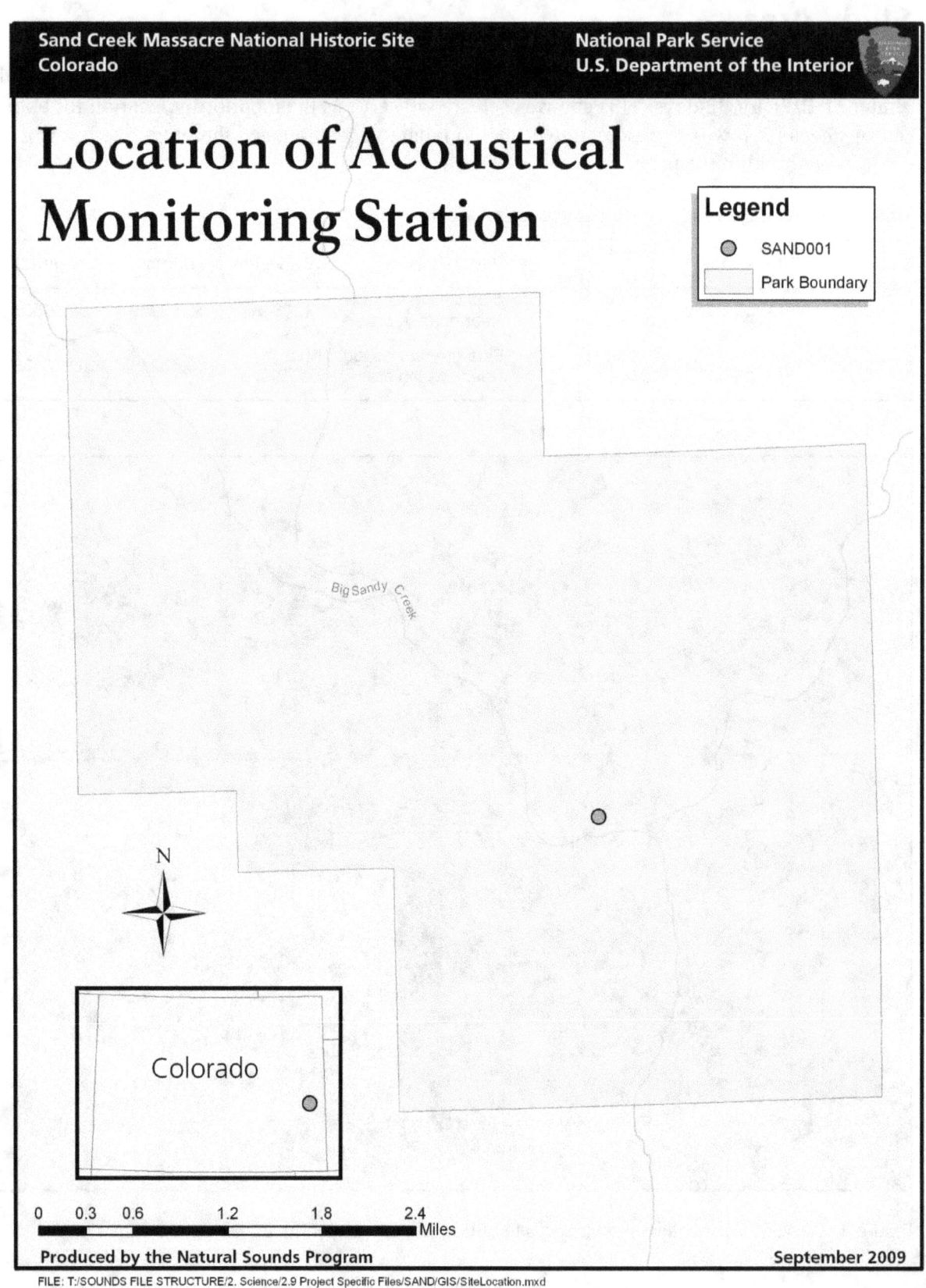

Figure 2. Location of SAND001

Methods

Equipment
Acoustical monitoring equipment is employed by various trades to determine noise levels in neighborhoods, near airports or roads, and in the workplace. While the Natural Sounds Program utilizes similar instruments, the harsh weather conditions encountered in national parks, long measurement periods, and possibility of wildlife encounters demand that the NSP develop a unique configuration. The system deployed at SAND included a Type 1 sound level meter (SLM) and a ½" prepolarized, random-incidence, condenser microphone. The Larson Davis 831 sound level meter collected 33 1/3 octave sound pressure level measurements (in dB) every second from 12.5 Hz to 20,000 Hz, which encompasses the nominal range of human hearing. The microphone was deployed in an environmental housing with a wind screen at approximately 1.5 meters above ground (a close approximation of the average height of the human ear). In addition to acoustical information, the SLM was configured to accept instantaneous wind speed, wind direction, temperature, and humidity, in real-time, from attached sensors.

Monitoring period
The variability of sound pressure levels over time and space in national parks is still not well understood. Each additional dataset gathered provides insight into natural variability. The monitoring period used for collection of these data is based on a preliminary statistical study that evaluated long-term datasets from Bryce Canyon National Park and Arches National Park. It was determined that a 25 day monitoring period in either winter or summer months would limit sound pressure level uncertainty to <3 dB (Iyer 2005). It is widely accepted that this is the threshold at which the average, healthy, human ear can detect noise level changes, when actively engaged in listening (Hendriks 1998). In addition to this study, logic dictates that a 25 day monitoring period would be sufficient to capture the inevitable variation in weather patterns in national parks.

Calculation of Metrics
There is no single metric that can be used to characterize the physical sound resources at a particular location (referred to as the *acoustical environment*), so a suite of metrics is employed. Acoustical studies in National Parks incorporate sound pressure level data (SPL), frequency data, audibility data, source identification data, and meteorological data. Perhaps the most fundamental descriptors used are existing ambient (L_{50}) and natural ambient (L_{nat}) sound levels. The L_{50} represents the median SPL, and encompasses spectra (in dB) drawn from the full dataset (although seconds with corresponding wind speeds > 5m/s are excluded to prevent errors from microphone distortion). The natural ambient (L_{nat}) is an estimate of what the ambient levels for a site would be in the absence of all extrinsic (or anthropogenic) sources. Unlike the existing ambient, the natural ambient is comprised of spectra drawn from a subset of the original data. For a given hour (or other specified time period), L_{nat} is calculated to be the decibel level exceeded x percent of the time, where x is defined by the equation

$$x = \frac{100 - P_H}{2} + P_H,$$

and P_H is the percentage of samples containing extrinsic or anthropogenic sounds for the hour. For example, if human caused sounds are present 30% of the hour, x = 65, and the L_{nat} is equal to the L_{65}, or the level exceeded 65% of the time for that hour. One concern with this approach is that some loud natural sounds, such as thunder, might be removed from the data during calculation of natural ambient, and the resulting L_{nat} levels could be an under-estimate of true natural ambient sound levels. Although this is a valid concern, such events are rare, relative to the 25 day measurement period (NPS 2005). Therefore, removing these data would not likely have a significant impact on calculations of natural ambient sound levels. Because the audibility of both natural and anthropogenic sounds varies so widely across the day, L_x values are reported on an hourly basis.

Calculation of diel L_x values

The Natural Sounds Program uses a custom program called "Hourly Metrics" to generate L_x values from long term acoustical monitoring data. All of the values reported are medians. The software aggregates L_x values (L_{50}, L_{nat}, L_{90}) for each hour monitored, based on one-second L_{eq} data. Then, hourly percentile values (L_{50}, L_{nat}, L_{90} etc) are grouped by time category (daytime or nighttime), and the median of each time category is reported. For instance, for daytime L_{90}, all L_{90} values between 0700h and 1900h are calculated, the median of this set is reported.

Off-Site Sound Source Analysis

In 2005, the NPS drafted protocols for acoustic studies in National Parks, in cooperation with staff from the Volpe National Transportation Systems Center[3]. When these acoustic monitoring protocols were developed, the amount of power it took to run recording devices, and storage limitations of these devices, were such that continuous recordings could not be made. As an alternative, recordings were made every 2 minutes for 10 seconds. This sampling scheme was designed to ensure that events of interest (namely aircraft and vehicles) would be recorded. Since that time, audio recorders have become much smaller and require less power. In addition, storage devices with larger capacities have become readily available. Therefore, continuous audio recordings were collected during the 2009 and 2011 monitoring efforts at SAND.

The 2005 protocol also dictated that during the recommended 25-day monitoring period, investigators would conduct several hours of observer logging or recording playback (typically 16 hours per site) to determine the audible sources of noise. Continuous recording has allowed us the convenience of conducting these listening sessions in the office instead of in the field. Thus, NSP staff still listen to a subset of the audio data, using the 10 seconds per 2 minutes sampling scheme. When placed end-to-end, these 10 second samples constitute 2 hours of audio recordings. To reach an equivalent 16 hours of observer logging, we listen to 8 days of sub-sampled audio.

At sites where anthropogenic noise occurs infrequently (such as SAND001), NSP staff can further accelerate source identification using daily spectrograms generated from sound pressure level data. Spectrograms are plots which display sound level as a function of time and frequency.

---

[3] National Park Service. 2005. Acoustic and Soundscape Studies in National Parks DRAFT.

Because most anthropogenic sounds possess recognizable sound signatures, staff can quickly examine many samples within the measurement period, noting duration, frequency span, maximum level, and sound exposure level (SEL) of each noise event. However, for events with less distinctive sound signatures, corresponding audio files are played back through noise canceling headphones. When all events have been identified, NSP software calculates the total percent time anthropogenic sounds were audible. This information is then used to calculate the estimated natural ambient sound level for each hour, as discussed in the "Calculation of Metrics" section. To learn more about visual analysis techniques, see Appendix A.

Figure 3. An acoustical technician uses software to visually analyze type and duration of sound sources.

On-Site Listening

On-site listening is the practice of placing an observer near an acoustical monitoring station with a handheld Personal Digital Assistant (PDA). The observer listens for a designated period of time (generally one hour), and identifies all sound sources and their durations. On-site listening takes full advantage of human binaural hearing capabilities, and closely matches the experience of park visitors. Logistical constraints prevent comprehensive sampling by this technique, but selective samples of on-site listening provide a basis for relating the results of off-site listening to the probable auditory perception of events by park visitors and wildlife. On-site listening sessions are also an excellent screening tool for parks initiating acoustic environment studies. They produce an extensive inventory of sound sources, require little equipment or training, and can help educate park staff and volunteers.

Numerous one-hour periods of on-site listening were conducted at SAND in order to discern the type, timing, and duration of events during sound-level data collection. Staff recorded the beginning and ending times of all audible sound sources using custom-designed PDA software. These on-site listening sessions provided the basis for the calculation of metrics, including the period of time between noise events (average noise free interval [NFI]), percent time each sound source was audible, and maximum, minimum, and mean length (in seconds) of sound source events.

Figure 4. An acoustical technician tracks audible sound sources on a PDA during an on-site listening session.

Results

For comparison purposes, results from both summer and winter monitoring efforts will be covered in this section. Table 2 presents a quick summary of the type of data collected at each site.

Table 4. Summary of data collected at SAND from 2009-2011.

Site Name	SAND001	SAND001
Data collector	NPS	NPS
# Days of data	45	32
SPL meter	LD-831	LD-831
Frequency range collected	12.5-20000 Hz	12.5-20000 Hz
Continuous audio	Yes	Yes
Electronic noise floor[4]	6.0 dB	13.2 dB
Dates of collection	7/13/09 - 8/26/09	1/13/11 - 2/14/11
# Days visual analysis	8	8
# On-site listening sessions	1	4

On-site listening

The following two tables (Table 3 and Table 4) display the results of on-site listening sessions during the summer and winter seasons. Each audible sound source is listed in the first column. Percent time audible, or PA, is the second column. The third column, Max, reports the maximum event length (in mm:ss) among the sessions for each sound source. Likewise, mean event and min event columns report the mean and minimum length of events. SD reports the standard deviation among event lengths, and count reports the number of times that each sound source was audible. The last row in the table, noise free interval (NFI), is a metric which describes the length of time between extrinsic or human-caused events.

At first glance, it would seem that human activity near the study site increased dramatically in the winter, when compared to the summer results. However, ambient acoustical conditions during on-site logging can have a large effect on the percent time audible of non-natural sound sources. Wind speed during the single summer listening session was particularly high. Thus, summer listeners were faced with acoustical masking from rustling leaves (100%), birdsong (31%), and insect sounds (100%), while the winter listeners heard less wind (50%) and infrequent birdsong (23%). Because fewer masking sounds existed during the few hours when staff were on site, winter listeners heard more non-natural events for longer periods of time. This

---

[4] The specifications for the LD 831 and microphone used at these sites indicate that the overall system noise floor is about 17 dB.

is a common and paradox in national parks: oftentimes, the quietest sites are the most vulnerable to noise intrusions.

Table 5. Summary of on-site audible sources for one hour at SAND001 summer. n=1.

Sound Source	PA	Max Event (mm:ss)	Mean Event (mm:ss)	Min Event (mm:ss)	SD Event (mm:ss)	Count
Jet, commercial	13.0	2:03	0:46	0:18	0:30	10
Aircraft, Propeller	8.0	1:34	0:55	0:26	0:34	5
Wind	0.0	0:04	0:04	0:04	0:00	1
Bird	31.0	3:59	0:54	0:10	1:21	21
Insect	100.0	60:0	60:0	60:0	0:00	1
Wind-induced natural sound	100.0	57:9	29:58	2:46	38:27	2
All Aircraft	20.4					
All Non-natural Sources	20.4					
All Natural Sources	100.0					
Noise Free Interval		15:50	3:11	0:30	5:11	15

Table 6. Summary of on-site audible sources for one hour at SAND001 winter. n=4.

Sound Source Description	PA	Max Event (mm:ss)	Mean Event (mm:ss)	Min Event (mm:ss)	SD Event (mm:ss)	Count
Aircraft	3.0	4:15	3:26	2:36	1:10	2
Jet	73.0	20:13	4:35	0:10	4:09	38
Aircraft, Propeller	3.0	3:16	2:00	1:06	0:57	4
Non-natural Unknown	5.0	2:53	0:58	0:01	0:56	12
Wind	50.0	36:19	4:09	0:11	7:09	29
Bird	25.0	5:09	0:44	0:01	1:03	82
Natural Other	2.0	1:51	0:42	0:05	0:37	6
Cracking or Popping Tree	0.0	0:03	0:02	0:02	0:01	9
All Aircraft	77.3					
All Non-natural Sources	82.1					
All Natural Sources	64.1					
Noise Free Interval		7:49	1:26	0:01	1:49	38

Off site analysis

While on-site listening results serve as a snapshot of what a visitor might experience in one hour at the site, off site analysis provides a much wider picture of the acoustical environment over the long-term. Due to temporal variations in source audibility, results are reported by time category (e.g. day and night). The first column in the tables below (Table 5 and Table 6) presents the audibility results for all hours (00-23), while the remaining columns present audibility for different sections of the day and night. Finally, an average count of events per day is shown.

The lists of audible sound sources differed slightly across the two monitoring seasons. For instance, the privately-owned agricultural fields near the site were occupied by cows during the summer monitoring period, but were vacant in the winter. Additional differences in audibility can be traced directly to the seasonal management of the park. Maintenance activities such as grounds care and mowing (audible 1.0% of the time in the summer) were absent in the winter. Finally, some differences in sound source audibility simply reflected changing use of nearby parcels. The quiet winter conditions allowed NSP staff to identify the distant sound of an oil well pump jack located about 2 miles northeast of the study site. This sound was audible an average of 5.5% of the time between 7pm and 7am during the winter season, and not at all during the summer.

Despite seasonal differences, there are a few universal sound sources that can be compared between the two monitoring periods. Commercial jet traffic was surprisingly consistent across both seasons. Approximately 109 jets per day were audible about 24% of the time in the summer, while 110 jets were audible 22% of the time in the winter. This similarity of results suggests a consistently high level of air traffic over SAND, regardless of season. The park's proximity to Denver International Airport is one likely cause for this situation.

Only extrinsic noises were logged during audibility analysis. However, a number of remarkable biologic sounds were noted in the process. These included multiple great horned owls, western meadowlarks, bullfrogs, coyotes, and at least one unknown bat species. Recordings of these sounds can be made available to the park.

Table 7. Summary of off-site analysis for audible sound sources, SAND001 summer. n=8.

Sound Source	00h-23h	07h-18h	19h-06h	08h-15h	16h-07h	Avg # Events 00h-23h
Jet	24.0	30.5	17.5	30.2	20.9	108.6
Propeller	5.9	9.6	2.1	10.4	3.6	22.1
Non-natural unknown	4.3	2.4	6.2	2.4	5.3	11.2
Cow	1.1	0.6	1.6	0.0	1.6	2.6
Grounds care	1.0	2.0	0.0	3.0	0.0	1.2
Train	0.5	0.0	1.0	0.0	0.7	0.5
Vehicle	0.2	0.2	0.2	0.2	0.2	1.4
Motor	0.1	0.2	0.0	0.3	0.0	0.2
Helicopter	0.0	0.0	0.0	0.1	0.0	0.1
Voices	0.0	0.0	0.0	0.1	0.0	0.1
Total Vehicle	0.2	0.2	0.2	0.2	0.2	1.4
Total Aircraft	29.8	39.9	19.6	40.4	24.4	130.9
Total Non-Natural	36.5	45.0	28.1	45.7	31.9	148.2

Table 8. Summary of off-site analysis for audible sound sources, SAND001 winter. n=8.

Sound Source	00-23h	07-18h	19h-06h	08-15h	16-07h	Avg # Events 00h-23h
Aircraft, Unknown	0.1	0.1	0.1	0.2	0.0	0.4
Jet	22.1	27.9	16.3	25.2	20.5	110.6
Military Jet	0.2	0.3	0.1	0.4	0.1	1.4
Propeller	3.8	6.3	1.2	5.9	2.7	13.8
Helicopter	0.0	0.0	0.0	0.0	0.0	0.1
Vehicle	1.2	2.2	0.2	2.3	0.7	4.0
Backup beeper	0.1	0.2	0.0	0.3	0.0	1.4
Non-natural unknown	3.1	2.5	3.7	2.4	3.5	8.1
Pump	3.2	0.8	5.5	0.2	4.7	5.2
Total Aircraft	26.1	34.5	17.7	31.6	23.4	126.2
Total Vehicle	1.2	2.2	0.2	2.4	0.7	5.4
Total Non-natural unknown	3.1	2.5	3.7	2.4	3.5	8.1
Total Pump	3.2	0.8	5.5	0.2	4.7	5.2
Total Non-Natural	33.4	39.8	27.0	36.3	32.0	145.0

Metrics

In order to determine the effect that noise audibility has on the acoustic environment, it is useful to examine the median hourly exceedence metrics. On site and off site listening reveal types and characteristics of sound sources, but exceedence metrics allow us to put those ambient conditions in the context of the decibel (dB) scale. The logarithmic dB scale can be difficult to interpret, and the effects of a seemingly small change in sound pressure level (SPL) can be greater than anticipated. For example, if the ambient SPL is 30 dB, and a noise event raises the ambient to 33 dB (a 3 dB increase), the listening area for humans (as well as many birds and mammals) would be reduced by 50%. Increasing the ambient SPL an additional 3 dB (to 36 dB) would reduce the listening area by half again, to 25% of the initial area. Note however, that changes in SPL do not proportionately translate to changes in perceived loudness. The rate of change of loudness is complex and dependent on the stimulus itself (SPL, frequency, bandwidth, duration, background, etc.). At a minimum, each 10 dB increase in SPL causes a doubling of perceived loudness (Crocker, 1997, p.1481).

Figure 5 and Figure 6 show existing ambient levels and natural ambient levels at the study site in both seasons. The existing ambient (or median) level for each hour is marked by the upper limit of the gray boxes while natural ambient levels (L_{nat}) are marked by the lower limit of the gray boxes (see legend). These figures also show exceedence metrics L_{10} and L_{90}, which mark the average maximum and minimum levels over the month-long monitoring period. These results indicate that acoustical conditions at Sand Creek Massacre National Historic Site are considerably quieter in the winter than they are in the summer. In fact, some of the measured sound levels were at or near the noise floor (lowest recording limit) of the equipment during the nighttime and early morning hours (see hours 0, 1, 2, 3, 4, 22, and 23 in Figure 6). Higher summer nighttime sound levels are likely attributable to insects and other vocal nocturnal animals.

In both winter and summer, the daytime hours are the most affected by anthropogenic sounds. However, some human-caused sounds were still present during the evening hours. During the summer, the primary nighttime noise sources were jets and an unknown non-natural sound (see audibility results in Table 5). During the winter, the primary nighttime noise sources were jets and the sound of an oil pump (see audibility results in Table 6). In both seasons, jets were the most prevalent sound source.

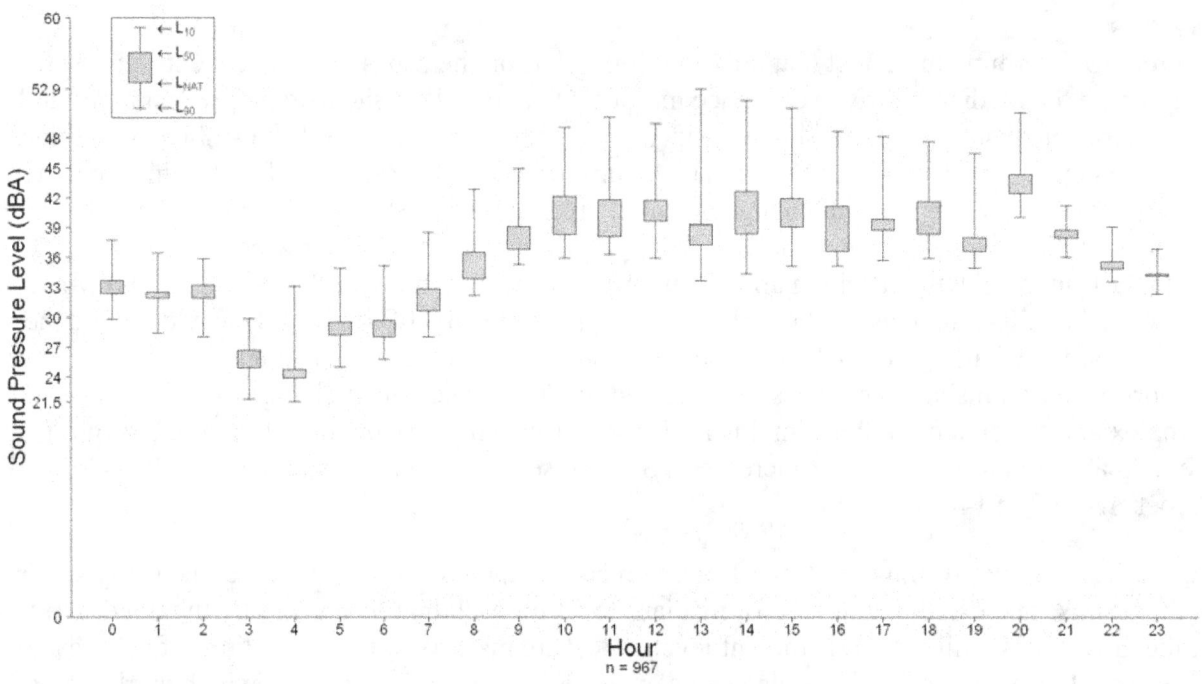

Figure 5. Median hourly exceedence metrics in dBA at SAND001 summer.

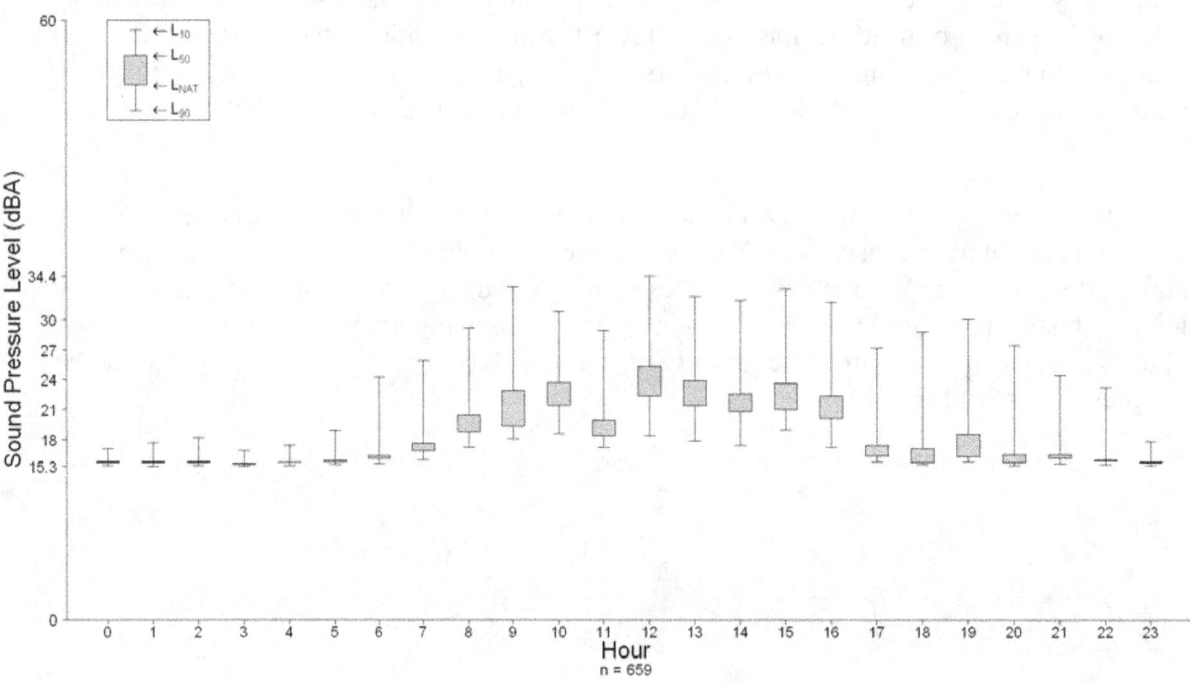

Figure 6. Median hourly exceedence metrics in dBA at SAND001 winter.

High frequency sounds (e.g. a cricket chirping) and low frequency sounds (e.g. transportation noise) often occur simultaneously, and do not always occur constantly throughout the day. Figure 7 and Figure 8 illustrate these concepts by dividing the full frequency spectrum into 33 smaller frequency bands (each encompassing a one-third octave range), and by plotting the daytime and nighttime SPL range for each band. The grayed area in the background of the graph represents sound pressure levels outside of the typical range of human hearing. The typical frequency ranges for transportation, conversation and songbirds are presented on the figure as examples for interpretation of the data. These ranges are estimates and are not vehicle-, species-, or habitat- specific, but do suggest possible sound sources. For instance, the obvious daytime peak in the high frequency bands on the summer plot is likely due to insects (audible 100 percent of the time during the on-site listening session), and birdsong (audible 31% of the time during the on-site listening session).

Plots such as these also provide some insight into the phenomenon of masking. Notice how bird sounds and transportation noise appear at different locations on the frequency spectrum (x axis) in Figure 7 and Figure 8. If two sounds are within similar or overlapping frequency ranges and one sound is louder than the other, some masking may occur. However, if the two sounds have the same dB level, they would not mask each other because they occupy different frequencies. It should be noted that there is evidence to suggest that the combined effect of vehicle noise, wind, and running water can mask distant aircraft, in some cases.

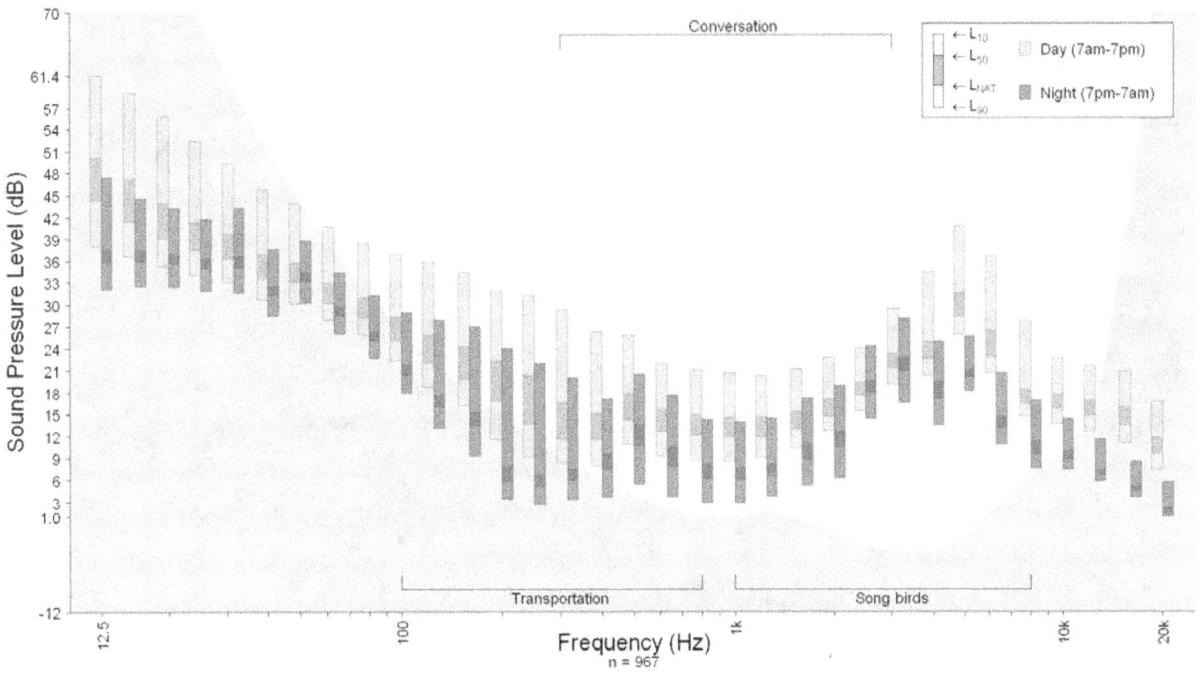

Figure 7. Day and night dB levels for 33 one-third octave bands at SAND001 summer

Notice in Figure 8 that the L_{90} (or the quietest 10% of the measured datapoints) for both daytime and nighttime dip into the gray shaded area. This means that at its quietest, SAND001 had sound levels (in certain frequencies) lower than can be perceived by the average human ear.

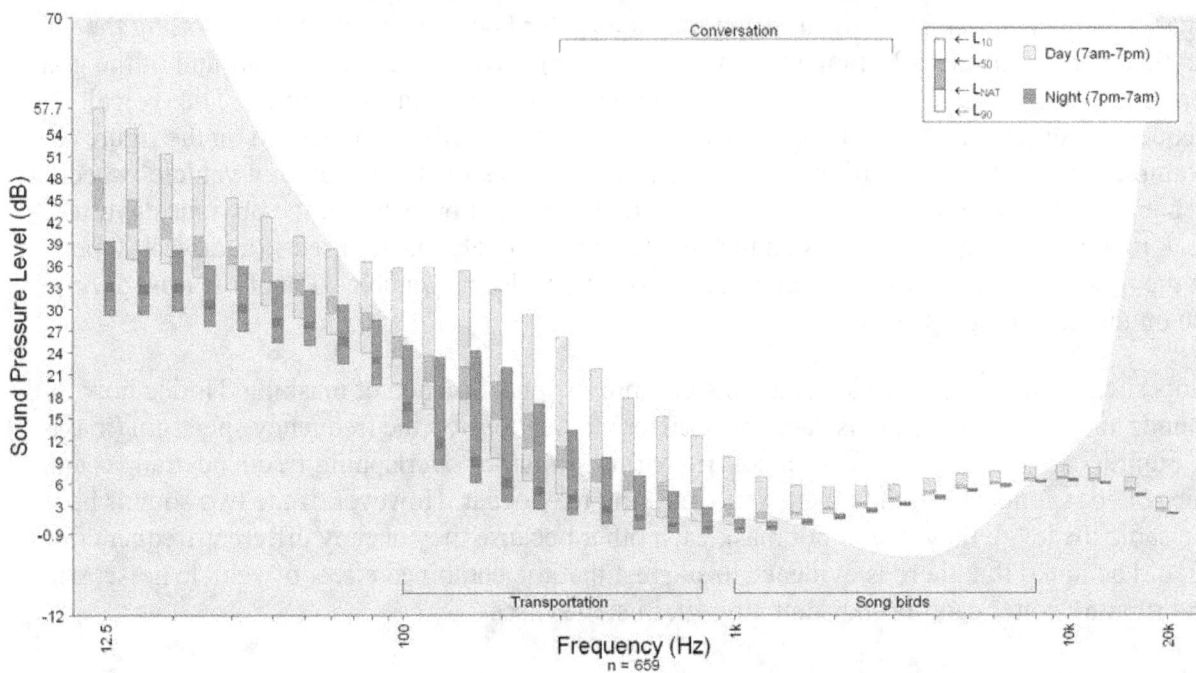

Figure 8. Day and night dB levels for 33 one-third octave bands at SAND001 winter

Conclusion

Acoustical monitoring in national parks not only permits us to gain insight into biological activity, but also allows us to determine the prevalence of extrinsic noise, and perhaps estimate its effects on visitors and wildlife. This study was successful in determining current acoustical conditions at Sand Creek Massacre National Historic site (SAND) over two seasons. Results included measures of existing ambient levels, calculations of sound source durations, and estimates of natural ambient levels. It was determined that human-caused sounds were audible an average of 36.5 percent of the time during the summer, and 33.4 percent of the time during the winter. Commercial jets were audible an average of 24 percent of the time during the summer and 22 percent of the time during the winter. The consistency of this aircraft audibility is likely attributable to the proximity of Denver International Airport. Nevertheless, monitoring results indicated that there are still periods of time of over 15 minutes or more during the daytime hours, where visitors can experience tranquility and solitude at SAND. Both existing and natural ambient conditions were remarkably quiet in the winter, when biological activity was at its lowest. Ambient conditions during the summer were elevated by natural sounds like wind rustling vegetation, birds, and insects.

A major impetus for this study was the development of the Colorado Air National Guard's (COANG) NEPA document for expansion of the Cheyenne Military Operations Area. NSP and the COANG are working together to document the nature and extent of impacts from the current level of military overflights. During the summer monitoring period, the COANG logged all flights conducted near the park. When compared against spectral data, only one of these flights was noticeable. This flight was conducted within 5 nautical miles of the park at 5,000 feet above ground level and registered 58 to 60 dB on the sound level meter and lasted for less than a minute. Though they were by no means the most frequent contributor of noise, military overflights were more frequently audible (about .02% of the day) during the winter.

The information presented in this report will be used to inform park managers, tribal representatives, and planners as they compile the upcoming general management plan, but it will also serve as a permanent record of what the park sounded like in 2009 and 2011. Sound pressure level data as well as continuous digital audio recordings will be stored at the Natural Sounds Program office for archiving purposes.

Literature Cited

Berglund, B., T. Lindvall, and D.H. Schwela (Eds.). 1999. HWO. Guidelines for community noise. World Health Organization, Geneva.

Dooling, R., and A. Popper. 2007. The effects of highway noise on birds. Environmental BioAcoustics LLC, Rockville, Maryland. Prepared for the California Department of Transportation. Available online at http://itvendors.dot.ca.gov/hq/env/bio/files/caltrans_birds_10-7-2007b.pdf

Haralabidis A.S., K. Dimakopoulou, F. Vigna-Taglianti, M. Giampaolo, A. Borgini, M. Dudley, G. Pershagen, G. Bluhm, D. Houthuijs, W. Babisch, M. Velonakis, K. Katsouyanni, L. Jarup. 2008. Acute effects of night-time noise exposure on blood pressure in populations living near airports. European Heart Journal Advance Access. Published online February 12, 2008. doi:10.1093/eurheartj/ehn013.

Haas, G.E., & T.J. Wakefield, 1998. National parks and the American public: A national public opinion survey on the national park system. Washington D.C. and Fort Collins, CO: National Parks and Conservation Association and Colorado State University.

McDonald, C. D., R.M. Baumgarten, and R. Iachan. 1995. Aircraft management studies: National Park Service Visitors Survey. HMMH Report No. 290940.12; NPOA Report No. 94-2, National Park Service, U.S. Department of the Interior.

National Park Service. 2005. Acoustic and Soundscape Studies in National Parks: Draft. National Park Service Natural Sounds Program, Fort Collins, C.O.

National Park Service. 2006a. Management Policy 4.9: Soundscape Management. . U.S. Department of Interior, National Park Service, Washington, D.C.

National Park Service. 2006b. Management Policy 8.2.3: Use of Motorized Equipment. . U.S. Department of Interior, National Park Service, Washington, D.C.

Appendix A: Visual analysis

The Natural Sounds Program used visual analysis to identify the type and duration of sounds at SAND001. Figure 9 shows one hour of sound pressure level data in the form of a spectrogram. A white box has been drawn around one commercial aircraft event.

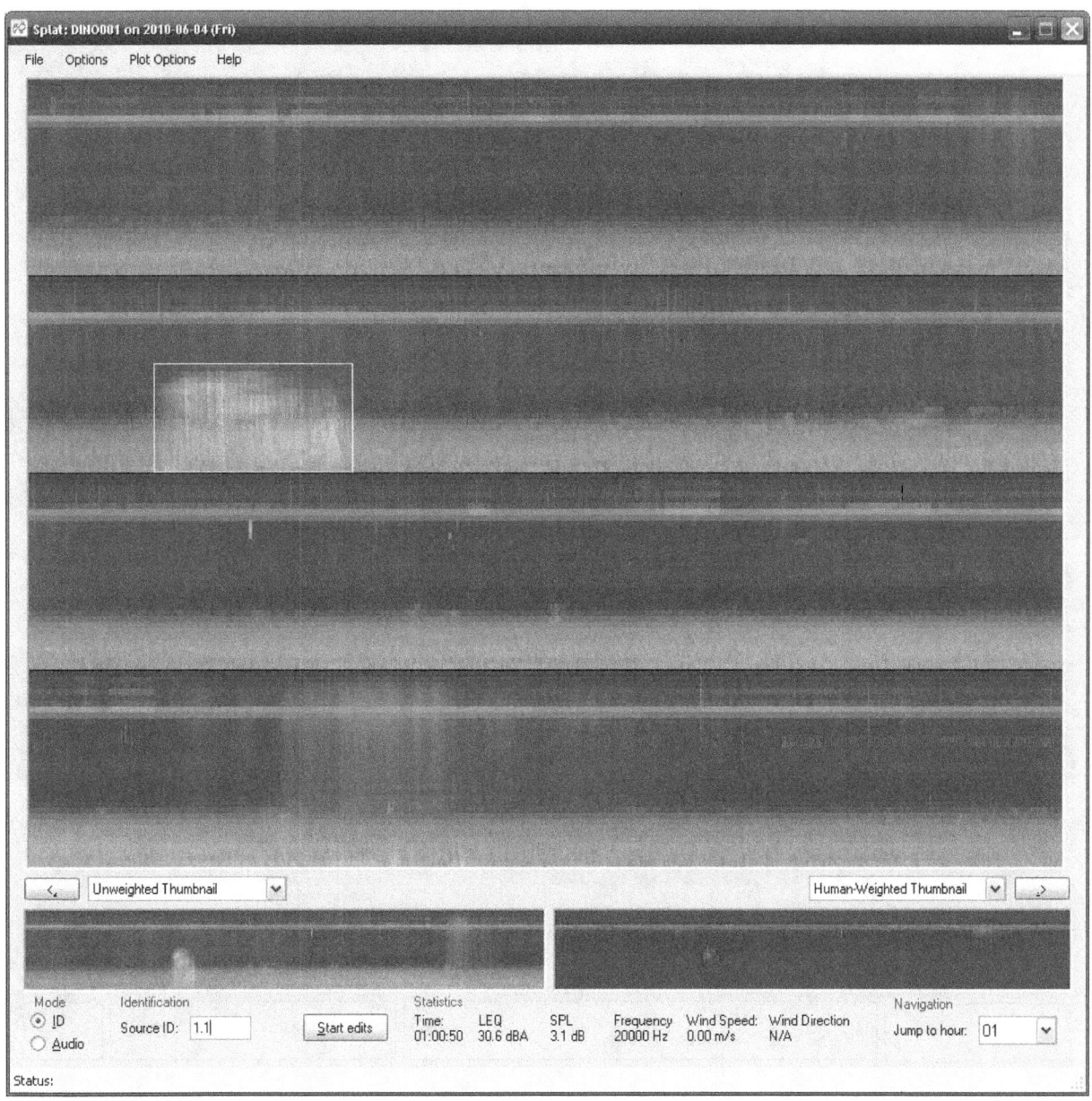

Figure 9. A demonstration of visual noise source analysis, using SPL annotation tool (SPLAT).

Appendix B: Glossary of Acoustical Terms

Acoustical Environment
The actual physical sound resources, regardless of audibility, at a particular location.

Alerting distance
The maximum distance at which a signal can be perceived. Alerting distance is pertinent in biological contexts where sounds are monitored to detect potential threats.

Amplitude
The instantaneous magnitude of an oscillating quantity such as sound pressure. The peak amplitude is the maximum value.

Atmospheric absorption
The part of transmission loss caused by conversion of acoustic energy into other forms of energy. Absorption coefficients increase with increasing frequency, and range from a few dB to hundreds of dB per kilometer within the spectrum of human audibility.

Audibility
The ability of animals with normal hearing, including humans, to hear a given sound. Audibility is affected by the hearing ability of the animal, the masking effects of other sound sources, and by the frequency content and amplitude of the sound.

A-weighted sound pressure level in decibels (dB(A) or dBA)
A frequency-based methodology used to account for changes in human hearing sensitivity as a function of frequency. The A-weighting network de-emphasizes the high (6.3 kHz and above) and low (below 1 kHz) frequencies, and emphasizes the frequencies between 1 and 6.3 kHz, in an effort to simulate the relative response of the human ear. A-weighted decibels are defined as ten times the logarithm to the base ten of the ratio of A-weighted squared sound pressure to the squared reference sound pressure of 20 μPa, the squared sound pressure being obtained with fast (F) (125-ms) exponentially weighted time averaging. Alternatively, slow (S) (1000-ms) exponentially weighted time averaging may be specified.

Decibel
Decibel is abbreviated dB, and is a logarithmic unit of sound-pressure-squared level; it is common practice, however, to shorten this to sound pressure level, when no ambiguity results from so doing. 0 dB represents the lowest sound level that can be perceived by a human with healthy hearing. The formula for computing decibels is:

$$L_{dB} = 10 \log_{10} \left(\frac{P_1}{P_0}\right)$$

Diel
A 24-hour period usually consisting of a day and the adjoining night.

Extrinsic Sound
Any sound not forming an essential part of the park unit, or a sound originating from outside the park boundary (also see Intrinsic Sound).

Frequency
Frequency equals the speed of sound divided by wavelength, and can be expressed in cycles per second, or Hertz (Hz). For a function periodic in time, the frequency is the reciprocal of the period, where the period is the smallest increment of an independent variable for which a function repeats itself (also see Hertz).

Ground attenuation
The part of transmission loss caused by interaction of the propagating sound with the ground.

Hearing Range (frequency)
By convention, an average, healthy, young person is said to hear frequencies from approximately 20Hz to 20,000 Hz.

Hertz (Hz)
A measure of frequency, or the number of pressure variations per second. A person with normal hearing can hear between 20 Hz and 20,000 Hz. Kilohertz (kHz) equals 1000 Hz.

Intrinsic sound
A sound which belongs to a park by its very nature, based on the park unit purposes, values, and establishing legislation. The term "intrinsic sounds" has replaced "natural sounds" in order to incorporate both cultural and historic sounds as part of the acoustic environment of a park (also see Extrinsic Sound).

Listening area
The area of a circle whose radius is the alerting distance. Listening area is the same as the 'active space' of a vocalization, with a listener replacing the signaler as the focus, and is pertinent for organisms that are searching for sounds.

Listening Horizon
The range or limit of one's hearing capabilities. Just as smog limits the visual horizon, so noise limits the acoustic horizon.

L_{eq}
Energy Equivalent Sound Level. The level of a constant sound over a specific time period that has the same sound energy as the actual (unsteady) sound over the same period.

L_x (Percentile –Exceeded Sound Level)
The A-weighted sound level equal to or exceeded by a fluctuating sound level x percent of a stated time period. For example, the symbol L10 represents that sound level which is exceeded 10 percent of the stated time period.

Masking (of a sound)

Interference with the detection of a sound due to the presence of another sound. More specifically, the number of decibels (dB) by which the intensity level of sound A must be raised above its threshold of audibility to be heard in the presence of a second sound, B. Sound A and sound B may be identical or may differ in frequency, complexity, or time.

Noise-Free Interval
The period of time between noise events (not silence).

Noise
Sound which is unwanted, either because of its effects on humans, its effect on fatigue or malfunction of physical equipment, or its interference with the perception or detection of other sounds.[5]

Noticeable
A signal that attracts the attention of an organism whose focus is elsewhere.

Off-site Listening
The systematic identification of sound sources using digital recordings previously collected in the field.

Percent Time Audible (PA)
The percent of time that a time-varying sound level may be detected in the presence of ambient sound as audible by the human ear.

Spectrum, power spectrum and spectral profile
The distribution of acoustic energy in relation to frequency. In graphical presentations, the spectrum is often plotted as sound intensity against sound frequency.
1/3 octave spectrum
Acoustic intensity measurements in a sequence of spectral bands that span 1/3 octave. The International Standards Organization defines 1/3rd octave bands used by most sound level meters (ISO 266, 1975). 1/3rd octave frequency bands approximate the auditory filter widths of the human peripheral auditory system.

Sound pressure level
Ten times the logarithm to the base ten of the ratio of the time-mean-square pressure of a sound, in a stated frequency band, to the square of the reference sound pressure in gases of 20 μPa, the threshold of human hearing. $SPL = 10Log_{10}(p^2/p_{ref}^2)$, where p^2 = time-mean-square sound pressure and p_{ref}^2 = squared reference sound pressure of 20 μPa.

---

[5] McGraw Hill Dictionary of Scientific and Technical Terms, online
http://www.accessscience.com/index.aspx

Spreading loss
More rigorously termed divergence loss. The portion of transmission loss attributed to the divergence of sound energy, in accordance with the geometry of environmental sound propagation. Spherical spreading losses in dB equal 20*log10(R/R0), and result when the surface of the acoustic wavefront increases with the square of distance from the source.

The Department of the Interior protects and manages the nation's natural resources and cultural heritage; provides scientific and other information about those resources; and honors its special responsibilities to American Indians, Alaska Natives, and affiliated Island Communities.

NPS 042/109120, August 2011

www.ingramcontent.com/pod-product-compliance
Lightning Source LLC
Chambersburg PA
CBHW081803170526
45167CB00008B/3312